Understanding

SUPREME
COURT CASES

Amanda Peterson

PowerKiDS press.

New York

Published in 2018 by **The Rosen Publishing Group, Inc.**
29 East 21st Street, New York, NY 10010

Cataloging-in-Publication Data
Names: Peterson, Amanda.
Title: Understanding supreme court cases / Amanda Peterson.
Description: New York : PowerKids Press, 2018. | Series: What's up with your government? |
   Includes index.
Identifiers: LCCN ISBN 9781538323328 (pbk.) | ISBN 9781538322369 (library bound) |
   ISBN 9781538323335 (6 pack)
Subjects: LCSH: United States. Supreme Court--Juvenile literature. | Constitutional law--
   United States--Cases--Juvenile literature. | United States. Supreme Court--Rules
   and practice--Juvenile literature. | Courts of last resort--United States--Juvenile literature.
Classification: LCC KF8742.P49 2018 | DDC 347.73'26--dc23

First Edition

Developed and Produced by Focus Strategic Communications, Inc.
   Project Manager: Adrianna Edwards
   Editor: Ron Edwards
   Design and Composition: Ruth Dwight
   Copy editors: Adrianna Edwards, Francine Geraci
   Media Researchers: Adrianna Edwards, Paula Joiner
   Proofreader: Francine Geraci
   Index: Ron Edwards, Maddi Nixon

Photo Credits: Credit Abbreviations: LOC Library of Congress; S Shutterstock; WC
Wikimedia Commons. Position on the page: T: top, B: Bottom, C: Center, L: left, R: right.
Cover TL: Zolnierek/S, TR: sirtravelalot/S, CL: Carsten Reisinger/S, B: W. Scott McGill/S; 1
TL: Zolnierek/S, TR: sirtravelalot/S, CL: Carsten Reisinger/S; 4: LOC/LC-USZ62-112705; 5:
User:King_of_Hearts/WC; 6: Architect of the Capitol; 7: USA.gov; 8: Everett Historical/S; 9:
LOC/LC-DIG-ppmsca-31804; 10: pisaphotography/S; 12: Brandon Bourdages/S; 14, 15: Everett
Historical/S; 16: Jerric Ramos/S; 17: Tinnaporn Sathapornnanont/S; 18: Steve Petteway,
Collection of the Supreme Court of the United States; 19: LOC/LC-U9-1027b-11; 20: Rob
Crandall/S; 21: The White House; 22: Rob Crandall/S; 23: The White House; 24: Erik Cox
Photography/S; 25: LOC/LC-2002698712; 27: Joseph Sohm/S; 28: Andrey_Popov/S; 29: Diego
G Diaz/S; Design Elements: Nella/S, tassita numsri/S.

Manufactured in the United States of America
CPSIA Compliance Information: Batch BW18PK: For Further Information contact
Rosen Publishing, New York, New York at 1-800-237-9932.

CONTENTS

THE SUPREME LAW OF THE LAND

SEGREGATION

Linda Brown (left), shown here in 1964, was a central figure in the landmark Supreme Court decision in 1954 outlawing school segregation.

The year was 1950. A girl named Linda Brown lived a few blocks from an elementary school. Still, every morning she took a bus to a more distant school. Black children were not allowed to attend school with white children. Linda's school was only for black children.

The National Association for the Advancement of Colored People (NAACP) asked Linda's father and several other black families to enroll their children in all-white schools. The schools said no.

The case was fought in the court system for several years. Finally, the Supreme Court of the United States said public schools could no longer be segregated.

BROWN V. BOARD OF EDUCATION

The NAACP worked with the parents to file a lawsuit. Their goal was to end racial segregation in schools.

The US District Court for Kansas heard the case. It sided with the Board of Education, and Topeka's schools would remain segregated. But Linda's father and the other **plaintiffs** were not finished. Their attorneys filed a **petition** to have the case heard by the Supreme Court.

On May 17, 1954, the Court ruled that children's race should not determine where they go to school. Segregation was deemed unconstitutional. It is one of the most important decisions in the Court's history.

Before the Supreme Court ruling of 1954, many states required educational segregation by race.

■ Required

□ No Legislation

■ Optional / Limited

■ Forbidden

Educational Segregation in the US Prior to *Brown v. Board of Education*

THE US CONSTITUTION

In the spring of 1787, men from across the United States gathered in Philadelphia, Pennsylvania. They had an important task: writing a constitution that described the government and laws of the United States.

Before the Constitution, the Articles of Confederation was the law of the land. The articles caused problems. States fought over bodies of water, trade, and taxation. The national government did not have much power. People worried the disagreements might turn violent.

The Founding Fathers signed the Constitution on September 17, 1787.

THREE BRANCHES OF GOVERNMENT

The Constitution united Americans. It created a strong **federal** government that had three branches: executive, legislative, and judicial. Each branch had its own powers. The Framers also made sure that a system of **checks and balances** was put in place. This ensures no branch is too powerful.

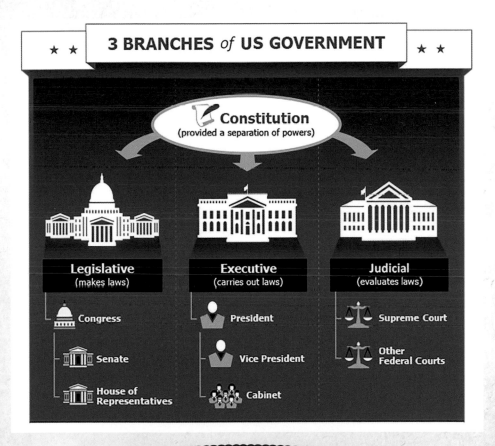

3 BRANCHES *of* US GOVERNMENT

Constitution
(provided a separation of powers)

Legislative (makes laws)	Executive (carries out laws)	Judicial (evaluates laws)
Congress	President	Supreme Court
Senate	Vice President	Other Federal Courts
House of Representatives	Cabinet	

The legislative branch of the government makes laws, the executive branch carries out laws, and the judicial branch evaluates laws.

THE JUDICIAL BRANCH

The judicial branch is responsible for interpreting laws and making sure that laws are followed. It is made up of a system of courts. The Framers stated there should be "one Supreme Court" and that Congress could create "inferior courts." Creating the court system was a gigantic task. It was not completed until 1789.

Framers of the Constitution

The Framers of the US Constitution included 55 delegates who attended the 1787 Constitutional Convention in Philadelphia. Among them were Benjamin Franklin, Alexander Hamilton, James Madison, and George Washington.

Many people consider James Madison (shown here) the Framer of the Constitution because he drafted the bulk of the document.

THE JUDICIAL ACT OF 1789

The Judicial Act of 1789 created the federal court system. The federal court system includes the Supreme Court and four types of lower courts. Those courts consist of appellate (appeals) courts, district courts, bankruptcy courts, and Article I courts.

The Judicial Act of 1789 also created the position of attorney general. The attorney general has the job of representing the United States government before the Supreme Court.

The first attorney general was Edmund Randolph of Virginia.

FAST FACT

After Edmund Randolph, 83 other individuals have served as attorney general.

★ ★

DISTRICT COURTS

District courts are also called trial courts. There are 94 district courts in the United States. Cases in district courts are heard by a judge and a jury.

The US District Court of New York, shown here, is located on Pearl Street in Lower Manhattan.

COURTS OF APPEAL

The United States has 13 courts of appeal. If someone does not agree with a verdict, or final decision, of a case heard in a district court, they might request an appeal. Three judges hear cases in the courts of appeal. There are no juries.

FAST FACT

Courts of appeal are also called appellate courts.

THE US FEDERAL COURT SYSTEM

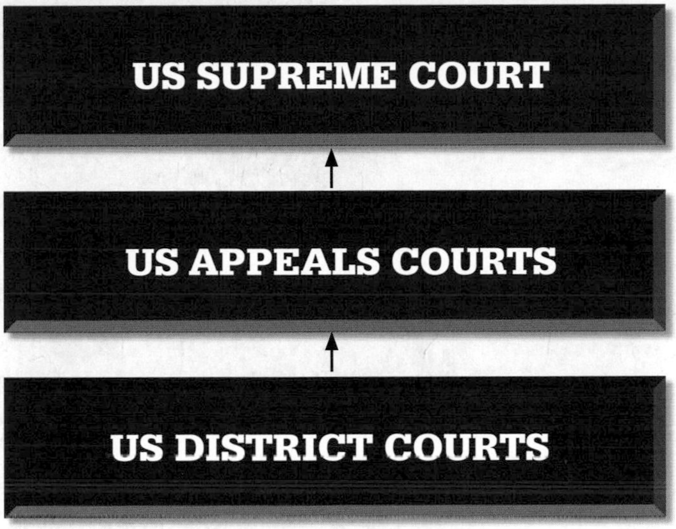

US SUPREME COURT

↑

US APPEALS COURTS

↑

US DISTRICT COURTS

THE STATE COURT SYSTEM

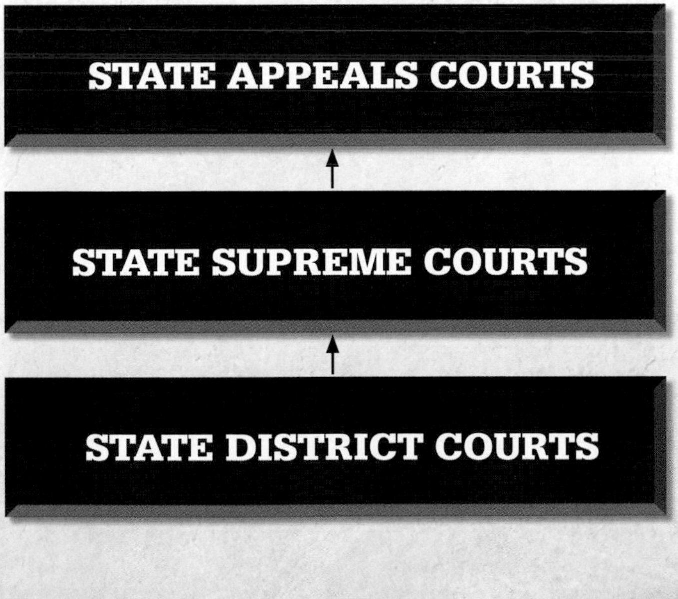

STATE APPEALS COURTS

↑

STATE SUPREME COURTS

↑

STATE DISTRICT COURTS

ONE SUPREME COURT

THE SUPREME COURT

There is only one Supreme Court. It mostly hears appeals of cases from the lower courts. Rulings made by its justices are final.

The United States Supreme Court is the highest and most powerful court in the land. It plays an important role in upholding the government as described in the Constitution. The Supreme Court can hear appeals from state courts as well as federal courts.

Equal Justice Under Law

The front of the federal Supreme Court building in Washington, DC, bears the engraved words "Equal Justice Under Law." This inscription is a motto for the American judicial system.

A carving of Liberty sits in the middle on a throne above the inscription, surrounded by eight other figures representing the ideals of American justice.

EQUAL JUSTICE UNDER LAW

POWER OF JUDICIAL REVIEW

The Supreme Court has the power of **judicial review.** This power protects the basic rights and values given to Americans by the Constitution. Justices of the Supreme Court review laws passed by Congress. If they "blow their whistle" and declare the law unconstitutional, it is no longer a law. Congress must try again. The Supreme Court can also check the powers of a president who has done something that violates, or goes against, the Constitution.

CHECKS AND BALANCES

The Supreme Court's powers are kept in check by both the executive and legislative branches. Justices are nominated by the president. The Senate must give its approval before a justice is officially **appointed** to the court. The House of Representatives has the power to **impeach** a justice.

PRESIDENT
Executive Branch
- President
- Executive and cabinet departments
- Independent agencies

Responsibilities: enforce laws

COURTS
Judicial Branch
- Supreme Court
- Courts of appeal
- District courts

Responsibilities: interpret the laws

CONGRESS
Legislative Branch
- House of Representatives
- Senate

Responsibilities: create laws

THE FIRST COURT

The first Supreme Court had five associate justices and one chief justice. George Washington appointed the first justices to the Court, including John Jay as the chief justice.

John Jay was one of the Founding Fathers. He was a lawyer from New York City and a Patriot. He signed the Treaty of Paris, which ended the American Revolutionary War.

John Jay was the first chief justice to serve on the Supreme Court. He was appointed by President George Washington in 1789. He served until 1795.

FAST FACT

The first meeting of the Supreme Court was supposed to be held on February 1, 1790. However, only three justices were present, so the whole thing had to be rescheduled for the next day! During its first term, the Court did not hear any cases.

The Jay Court

After Washington appointed John Jay as the first chief justice, he was unanimously confirmed by Congress almost immediately. James Wilson, William Cushing, John Rutledge, James Iredell, and John Blair were appointed as associate justices.

The first justices were all highly respected lawyers who had helped write the Constitution. They each represented different states: Blair was from Virginia, Cushing from Massachusetts, Iredell from North Carolina, Rutledge from South Carolina, and Wilson from Pennsylvania.

John Rutledge of South Carolina was one of the five men appointed by George Washington as associate justices of the first Supreme Court in 1789. He succeeded John Jay as the second chief justice in 1795.

A PLACE TO CALL HOME

The Supreme Court first met in New York City, which briefly served as the nation's capital. Then, in 1790, the nation's capital was moved to Philadelphia, and the Court met there for 10 years.

The Old Supreme Court chamber in Washington, DC, served as the meeting place of the US Supreme Court between 1810 and 1860.

Finally, in 1800, Washington, DC became the capital of the United States, and the Supreme Court moved there. The Court met in six different locations in the Capitol. Justices even met in private homes and taverns! From 1861 to 1935, the Court met in the Old Senate Chamber in the Capitol building.

A HOME OF ITS OWN

Former President William Taft became chief justice of the Supreme Court in 1921. He wanted the Court to have its own building. Finally, Congress agreed. The Court's first session in the Supreme Court Building was held on October 7, 1935.

The Supreme Court Building

The Supreme Court Building was designed by a famous architect named Cass Gilbert. Its size and appearance showed that the judicial branch was of equal importance to the legislative and executive branches. Construction began in 1932, and the building was completed in 1935.

Before the present building (pictured here) was completed in 1935, the Supreme Court met in many different locations.

FAST FACT

- The Supreme Court Building has its own police force.
- It is 92 feet (28 m) tall, 385 feet (117 m) long, and 304 feet (93 m) wide.
- It has a basketball court, the "Highest Court in the Land."
- In 2002, it took 24 hours to capture a fox that entered the building.

★ ★ ★ ★ ★ ★ ★ ★ ★ ★ ★ ★ ★ ★ ★ ★ ★ ★ ★ ★

JUSTICES OF THE COURT

Today's Supreme Court has nine justices. There are eight associate justices and one chief justice. Congress has the power to change the number of justices serving on the Court.

The nine Supreme Court justices in 2010 included (front row, left to right) Clarence Thomas, Antonin Scalia (deceased), Chief Justice John Roberts, Anthony Kennedy, and Ruth Bader Ginsburg. Back row (left to right): Sonia Sotomayor, Stephen G. Breyer, Samuel A. Alito, and Elena Kagan.

NOT ALWAYS NINE

Over the years, the number of Supreme Court justices has risen and fallen. The greatest number was 10. The smallest number was six. In 1869, the number of Supreme Court justices was set at nine, and it hasn't changed since.

YEAR	NUMBER OF SUPREME COURT JUSTICES
1789	6
1807	7
1837	9
1863	10
1866	7
1869	9

NO EXPERIENCE REQUIRED

Representatives, senators, and the president must meet strict age, residency, and citizenship requirements. You might be surprised to learn that the Constitution does not list specific qualifications for Supreme Court justices. A justice does not even need to have legal experience!

A Changing Court

In 1967, President Lyndon Johnson appointed Thurgood Marshall to the Supreme Court. He was the first African American justice to serve on the Court. He was the 96th justice of the Supreme Court.

Thurgood Marshall, shown here in 1957, served on the Supreme Court from 1967 to 1991. He died in January 1993.

FAST FACT

Thurgood Marshall's real name was Thoroughgood. When he was a child, he thought Thoroughgood was too difficult to spell, so he changed it to Thurgood!

APPOINTING JUSTICES

Article 2 of the Constitution gives the president the power to appoint justices to fill empty seats on the Supreme Court bench. When there is a vacant seat, the president and presidential advisors look for a **nominee**. They look for someone who has similar political opinions. This is important because Supreme Court justices are appointed for life. A president's influence will continue through the work of the justice even after the president is no longer in office.

Sandra Day O'Connor was appointed to the Supreme Court in 1981 by President Ronald Reagan. She was the first female justice and served until her retirement in 2006.

FAST FACT

As of January 2017, 112 justices had served on the Supreme Court.

★ ★ ★ ★ ★ ★ ★ ★ ★ ★ ★ ★ ★ ★ ★ ★ ★ ★

SENATE CONFIRMATION

The Senate **Judiciary** Committee meets with the nominee in a meeting called a special hearing. During the hearing, the nominee answers tough questions. When it is done, the committee shares its opinion with the full Senate. The Senate then votes to confirm or deny the nominee.

PARTY CONFLICT

In March 2016, President Barack Obama nominated Merrick Garland to replace Justice Antonin Scalia, who had died the previous month. The Senate failed to move to confirm the candidate and the clock ran out.

Newly elected President Donald Trump (left) nominated Neil Gorsuch as Supreme Court Justice in January 2017. Gorsuch was confirmed on April 7, 2017.

THE CHIEF JUSTICE

The chief justice position is not only in charge of the Supreme Court. The chief justice is also considered the head of the Judicial Branch of government.

A DEMANDING JOB

The chief justice is in charge of the Court at public and closed sessions. They lead closed-door meetings where the justices review cases. This gives the chief justice influence over the topics that are discussed.

John Roberts Jr. is the 17th and current chief justice of the Supreme Court.

FAST FACT

Since the Supreme Court first met in 1790, there have been only 17 chief justices. The current chief justice, John Roberts Jr., was appointed by President George W. Bush in 2005. Roberts was only 50 years old at that time, so he could hold the position for a long time.

ROLE OF THE CHIEF JUSTICE

The chief justice is the boss of the Supreme Court. They get to decide the agenda of the Court weekly meetings where future cases are accepted or rejected for review. That person often sets the tone for discussions and influences the direction of these discussions.

ONLY ONE VOTE

Despite all of the prestige and authority of the role, the chief justice still has only one vote, just like the eight associate justices, on any legal matters. When the Court makes a ruling, it decides who will write the **opinion**.

Every four years, the chief justice administers the oath of office at the president's inauguration.

On January 20, 2017, Chief Justice John Roberts (bottom right) administered the oath of office to newly elected President Donald J. Trump.

THE WORK OF THE COURT

SITTINGS AND RECESSES

The Supreme Court hears cases starting the first Monday of October. The Court usually hears cases through late June or early July. This is called a **term**.

The Supreme Court Chamber. When the Court is in session, this is where cases are heard.

A term has sittings and recesses. A sitting is when justices hear cases and deliver their opinions. Recesses are when justices write opinions, review cases, and research and prepare **briefs** for upcoming cases. Each period lasts about two weeks, and they alternate throughout the term.

PUBLIC SESSIONS

Supreme Court hearings are open to the public. Each court day begins at 10 a.m. and lasts until 3 p.m., with a one-hour lunch break at noon. As a result, the Court sits for only four hours each day. In addition, the Court does not sit on Thursdays and Fridays.

THE COURT IS IN SESSION

When the Court is in session, oral arguments are heard on Mondays, Tuesdays, and Wednesdays. Hearings are usually held in the morning, beginning at 10:00 a.m.

THE COURT IS IN RECESS

When the Court is in recess, the justices are still hard at work. They read and prepare for upcoming cases. They may write opinions. Justices also spend time looking at petitions to decide which cases should be added to their **docket**.

The Officers of the United States Supreme Court

Without officers, the Supreme Court would have a hard time performing its functions. These officers include the counselor to the chief justice, who is appointed by the chief justice. Other officers include the clerk, the librarian, the marshal, and the reporter of decisions, who are appointed by the Court. All others are appointed by the chief justice in consultation with the Court.

This December 1864 photograph shows the US Supreme Court with the nine justices. Chief Justice Salmon P. Chase is in the middle, and Court Clerk D.W. Middleton appears on the far left side (standing).

TYPES OF JURISDICTION

The Supreme Court has two types of **jurisdiction**: appellate and original. Virtually all of the cases heard by the Supreme Court are appeals from lower courts. In appellate cases, the Supreme Court reviews the decisions made by lower courts. Original jurisdiction means that the Supreme Court is the first and only court to hear the case. Such cases usually involve states or ambassadors. There are no appeals to Supreme Court rulings; its judgment is final.

COURT JURISDICTIONS

ORIGINAL JURISDICTION

- Refers to the court that hears the case for the first time.
- Sometimes called trial courts (state) or district courts (federal).
- Rarely does the Supreme Court function as an original court.

APPELLATE JURISDICTION

- Courts have the power to review cases from a lower court (original) and decide whether errors were made.
- Sometime called appellate courts (state) or courts of appeal (federal).
- Decisions by the Supreme Court are final and cannot be appealed.

FAST FACT

Individuals, companies, and governments who do not agree with a lower court's decision can petition the Supreme Court to review their case. This usually happens through a writ of certiorari, or a request for justices to review the decision.

★ ★

SELECTING CASES

Justices review about 150 petitions each week. They must be extremely selective. The justices discuss the petitions in a conference room. The only participants are the justices—no one else is allowed in the room.

The chief justice leads the meeting. They are the first to offer an opinion and cast a vote. The associate justices speak and vote in order of seniority. Four justices must vote to move a petition forward.

Being Selective

The Supreme Court receives between 7,000 to 8,000 petitions each year! Over the course of one term, justices will hear only about 80 cases. Sometimes justices rule more according to their personal beliefs than the Constitution. Thurgood Marshall, the Supreme Court's 96th justice, famously said: "You do what you think is right and let the law catch up."

Supreme Court justices should always keep the Constitution in mind when they review cases.

HEARING A CASE

When in session, the Supreme Court usually hears two cases a day. Each case lasts one hour.

JUSTICES' CONFERENCE

The justices' conference is held in absolute privacy. At the beginning of the meeting, the justices shake hands. This is done to show that even if divided in their opinions, the justices work together to serve the country. After reviewing petitions, they discuss hearings.

The United States Supreme Court is at the heart of the American justice system.

WRITING OPINIONS

A justice's vote will place them in the majority opinion or in the dissenting opinion. One of the justices will write an opinion explaining the decision of the majority (at least five justices out of nine). A dissenting opinion is written by a justice who does not agree with the majority.

Protecting Americans

Today, Americans are divided about many issues. Immigration, education, women's health, marriage equality, and gun ownership are often in the news. Many of those issues are debated in courtrooms across the country. Some of these cases will ultimately make it to the Supreme Court.

The work of the Supreme Court helps protect Americans' freedom of speech.

The work of the Supreme Court is extremely important. The justices work tirelessly to make sure that the Constitution is respected and upheld. In doing so, they protect Americans' freedoms and rights.

GLOSSARY

appoint — to give someone a specific job

brief — a summary

checks and balances — a system that allows each branch of a government to change or veto acts of another branch in order to prevent any one branch from having too much power

docket — a list of cases that will be heard

federal — a form of governance in which power is shared between a central government and state governments

impeach — to remove someone from public office for breaking the law

judicial review — decision by the US Supreme Court on whether a law or executive order abides by the US Constitution

judiciary — a system of courts and laws

jurisdiction — the power to interpret laws

nominee — a person who is chosen as a candidate for a position or title

opinion — a formal statement from a judge or court of the reasons for a legal decision

petition — an official written request to have something reviewed

plaintiff — the complaining party in a trial or lawsuit

term — a fixed period of time

FURTHER INFORMATION

BOOKS

Jacobs, Thomas A. and Jacobs, Natalie C. *Every Vote Matters: The Power of Your Voice, from Student Elections to the Supreme Court*. Minneapolis: Free Spirit Press, 2016.

Loria, Laura. *What Is the Judicial Branch?* New York: Britannica Educational Publishing, 2016.

Manger, Katherine. *The US Constitution*. New York: Britannica Educational Publishing, 2017.

Roland, James. *Ruth Bader Ginsburg: Iconic Supreme Court Justice*. Minneapolis: Lerner Publications, 2016.

Rubin, Susan Goldman. *Brown v. Board of Education: A Fight for Simple Justice*. New York: Holiday House, 2016.

ONLINE

PowerKids Press has developed an online list of websites related to the subject of this book. This site is updated regularly. Please use this link to access the list:

www.powerkidslinks.com/wuwyg/supremecourt

INDEX